Poland in Play: Stories and Skits for ESL

Barry Nicholson

Starhands Publishing

CONTENTS

LIST OF PLAY SCRIPTS

Introduction

Welcome to Poland!

Poland is a fascinating and diverse country, perfectly located in the centre of Europe. In this book you will find sixteen stories from Poland's rich cultural history. Importantly, each story is accompanied by a play script designed for young learners. Children and teens will enjoy acting out the skits, and will wake up to the joys of Polish stories through practical drama and literature.

Stories and tales were initially oral, then written forms were passed down from generation to generation, from grandfather to grandson, from grandmother to granddaughter. As technology developed with the use of printed, audio and electronic media, the tales have come to be more widely distributed and appreciated.

With this in mind, it is the aim of this book to enlighten the reader and their students of Poland's rich heritage by presenting a variety of stories and skits grouped according to theme. These stories remind us of the many traditions at work within the Polish nation in relation to its early Kings, rulers, maidens and dragons.

Play, Story and Skit

A few words in the book's title need defining: play, story and skit. The definitions have been drawn from various online dictionaries (see the reference list at the back of the book for details).

Play: In a theatrical sense, it is a piece of writing intended to be acted in a theatre or similar place of performance; it is a dramatic work for stage or to be broadcast. An intriguing alternative definition sees 'play' as a light or brisk, constantly changing movement, as in 'a play of light'; or on an even higher level as freedom of action or activity, as in 'a full play of the mind'. Whereas I do not expect our students to encounter this higher state of being, it would, however, be nice if their creative juices were squeezed and stretched a little.

Story: We often ask our students to write a story or order a sequence of events so that they make sense, and we usually use the past simple to achieve this. Essentially, a 'story' is a narrative, either true or fictional, designed to interest, amuse, or instruct the reader; and this is often a connected series of events that can be either true or imagined.

Skit: A 'skit' is a satirical or humorous story or sketch, especially one done by amateurs. It derives from the word 'sketch', and is often a comedic segment of a show or performance that often makes a joke of something. Certainly this element of humour is a theme that crops up throughout this book, and your children or teens will no doubt be eager to tap in to this valuable way of viewing the world at large.

A lot of the definitions suggest some kind of public performance, for example on TV or radio. Though I realise that this is beyond the capability of most of us in the classroom, it may be possible to experiment with a video camera or other audio-visual recording device as resources and technology allow. Failing that, a well-rehearsed public performance will certainly do!

Myth, Legend and Tale

You will also encounter the terms *myth*, *legend* and *tale* throughout the book. A 'myth' is a traditional story, usually with some historical basis, that points to the history, sociology or origin of a particular people. It typically involves supernatural beings or events, and embraces beliefs, concepts and ways of questioning to make sense of the world.

Similarly, 'legend' is a very old story (or set of stories) from long ago that is not always historical or true. They are unverifiable and handed down by tradition. Though debated and disputed many times, they are popularly accepted.

Finally 'tale' is a narrative that tells some real or imaginary event or story, and it is often invented or difficult to believe. In children's books it often starts with "Once upon a time...", though I have made the conscious decision *not* to start any of the stories in this way!

Scope and Style

This book is primarily aimed at parents and teachers and their child or children, but there is also much of interest to the general reader. The stories and skits are written in a simple and enjoyable way, but do not patronise the reader or student.

Thankfully English is an art, not a science; it is descriptive rather than prescriptive; it is a creative and cultural act. Throughout, the English language is taken as a creative being; an abstract entity that can be neither seen nor heard except in its manifestation as the written word or spoken utterance. This is expressed no more so than in a short play or skit. And, as Shakespeare would have it, "all the world's a stage, and all the men and women merely players". ('As You Like It' Act II Scene VII).

I want to motivate and inspire – that means teachers and parents as well as children and teens – and it is in this light that the book has been written. Though it does not claim to be *the* answer, or even *an* answer, the book does claim to be *a way*, a way to approach your lessons or study period through literature, stories and drama.

The question is really one of motivation, of getting students motivated to study, and to help them help their peers to success too. The skills our youngsters get in these early days will help propel them into the future – their future – towards high school, university and beyond. As they progress through time, the study skills, methods and motivation techniques we show them now will stick with them and be added to and developed by them; education, drama and story-telling skills that will stay with and guide them, that they themselves can pass on to others.

Students can then progress in their studies with purpose and confidence.

Structure and Layout

The structure is simple: each unit follows the same basic pattern. After the title there is a short summary of the story. Avoid the summary if you don't want the spoiler effect; read it carefully if you want to skip the story and go straight to the play script.

Then the story is told, mostly in past simple and in prose. It is designed to be read either in one's head or out loud, perhaps before an audience or class of students.

This is followed by three further sections, intended to develop comprehension and extension of the story as required. First there is a vocabulary section, where some potentially new or difficult words from the text are defined. Second comes the short section 'Did You Know?' which hits the reader with three short facts about the story or its context.

A third and final section, 'What Do You Think?', encourages parents and students alike to express their own opinions on the comings and goings of the story. The section encourages talking and interaction. How you set it up is up to you, but I'd suggest following the well-worn pattern of putting students into pairs or groups, perhaps with one person nominated as group leader. After this a plenary can be held in open-class format: within this you or the students can write any ideas on the board or in notebooks; or you could keep it purely auditory in traditional discussion style. For these lessons, or for parents working with their own children, encourage longer, not one-word answers.

Then the play script itself. First, there is a list of characters that appear in the play; then the setting (giving ideas for scenery and props, if these are to be included); then the script.

As a parent or teacher, it is your creative juices that are equally as important as the children's, and so you should feel free to adapt or add to the presented materials if you judge it to be correct, according to your opinion, resources, and working environment.

The Stories

The stories are divided into four main themes:

- ❖ Dragons, animals, monsters and spirits;
- ❖ Kings, Queens and Royalty;
- ❖ Common people;
- ❖ Places and things.

Each theme presents four stories (and, so, four plays or skits). In more detail the sixteen units are:

1. The Dragon of Krakow:

In a cave on the River Vistula lived a dragon who should never be disturbed. However some youths disturbed the dragon and it became very angry. A villager named Krakus managed to slay the dragon by baiting its food, making it drink until it exploded. Krakus was made leader of the prosperous city of Krakow.

2. The Obra Water Monster:

River Obra is home to a giant monster who attacks small animals and boats. But is it really just a giant catfish?

3. Rusalka:

Rusalka is a type of dangerous tree-dwelling spirit whose power comes from her beauty. She lives near lakes and forests in sparse areas.

4. The Mermaid of Warsaw:

While a prince was hunting he came across a mermaid who directed him to a cottage in a clearing. He met a young woman who had twin babies. He gave the land to her and told her to plant crops – thus starting the city of Warsaw.

5. King Boleslaw and his Knights:

Boleslaw and his Knights supposedly lie in waiting in a cave in the Tatra Mountains should Poland ever need them. The tale is similar to the story 'The Sleeping Knights' (Chapter 8).

6. The Queen of the Baltic:

Jurata, the Queen of the Baltic, had a palace made of amber at the bottom of the sea. She loved fish, and so decided to punish a fisherman. But when she saw how handsome he was she declared her love for him. A jealous God destroyed her palace, and the Queen of the Baltic and her lover both died.

7. The Legend of Wanda:

Wanda was a wise and good Queen and led a proud Poland. A German Prince, Rytigier, tried to blackmail her into marrying him but instead of giving in she drowned herself in the River Vistula.

8. The Sleeping Knights:

A stranger got the village blacksmith to make a golden horseshoe, and led him to a cave to fit the shoe. Inside there was an army of sleeping knights and horses who would only wake in times of trouble. The tale claims that the bravest knights never die, but are asleep in this cave beneath Mount Pisana.

9. Janosik: Polish Robin Hood:

Janosik was a Polish Robin Hood: he robbed from the rich and gave to the poor. A major difference is that he had magical powers. He and his men lived in the Tara Mountains on both the Polish and Slovak sides.

10. The Trumpeter of Krakow:

Krakow was threatened with an invasion, so the trumpeter played a tune over and over to warn the city. However, one arrow hit him and he died. To honour this sacrifice, the tune is played hourly even to this day.

11. The Three Brothers:

Three brothers, Lech, Czech and Rus, inherited both land and wealth, but their lands were overpopulated. So, they set off together, and then in their own three directions, to found lands of their own. Lech stayed in the land that is now modern-day Poland.

12. Jadwiga and her Apron of Roses:

Some people will go to great lengths to help others and make sure they are fed and watered. Queen Jadwiga was one such person and, as legend has it, she hid food in her apron and sneaked out of her castle nightly to give to the poor.

13. How the Pussy Willow got its Fur:

Three cute kittens fell into a river but were saved by some nearby pussy willow trees who helped them back to shore.

14. What is the National Flower of Poland?

There is an official national flower, the Corn Poppy (or red poppy). However, there are some other contenders, including sunflowers, roses, carnations, St John's Wort, and some more unusual flowers such as the Siberian Iris, Globe Flower, Ostrich Fern, or the elusive 'fire flower'.

15. The Three Gifts:

This is a long tale about the fate of a sister, step-sister, a brother, and a wicked step-mother who, through fate and fortune, got involved with the royal family with differing outcomes.

16. The Legend of the Golden Duck

A talking duck gave money to Jacob on condition that he only spent it on himself. However, he gave one gold coin to a poor beggar upon which all his wealth and goods disappeared.

Visiting the Places in this Book

As I sit and write this book I am in Krakow. It is a lovely place and I would recommend anyone to visit, especially with children. They will love Wawel Castle or the fire-breathing statue of the Krakow Dragon, for example. Most of the stories in this book have a geographical location, or can at least be tied to some part of Poland. As such, most places can be visited with the effect that the stories and plays you have studied come to life!

Apart from Krakow, you could make a visit to the Chopin Institute (Ostrogoski Pialace) in Warsaw and see a statue of the Golden Duck in a small pond near the palace. Or how about a day trip to the Baltic Sea to try and find a fragment of jade from Queen Jutra's palace? In the time-lost villages around Krakow you can almost see Jadwiga carrying her apron of food to the poor.

You may be more reluctant to visit the spooky Koscieliska Valley and Mount Pisana, where knights and stallions are said to sleep. Or the dark forests and deep lakes of Western Pomerania and Lubuskie, where the beautiful man-eater Rusalka once roamed (still roams?).

Maps of Poland, its major cities, and its most popular national parks and mountains are widely available from bookshops or the nearest tourist information centre. They vary in quality and scale, but most can be interpreted by an English-speaker (even without a working knowledge of Polish!). Larger post offices also have information, and, as ever, there is a wealth of information online (the references section at the back gives some starting places). And don't forget the helpful receptionist at your hotel.

What more can I say? Enjoy this collection of diamonds from Poland's past, and all things considered your children and teens will wake up and enjoy them too.

Barry Nicholson
Krakow 2017

Part 1

Dragons, Animals, Monsters and Spirits

(1)

The Dragon
of
Krakow

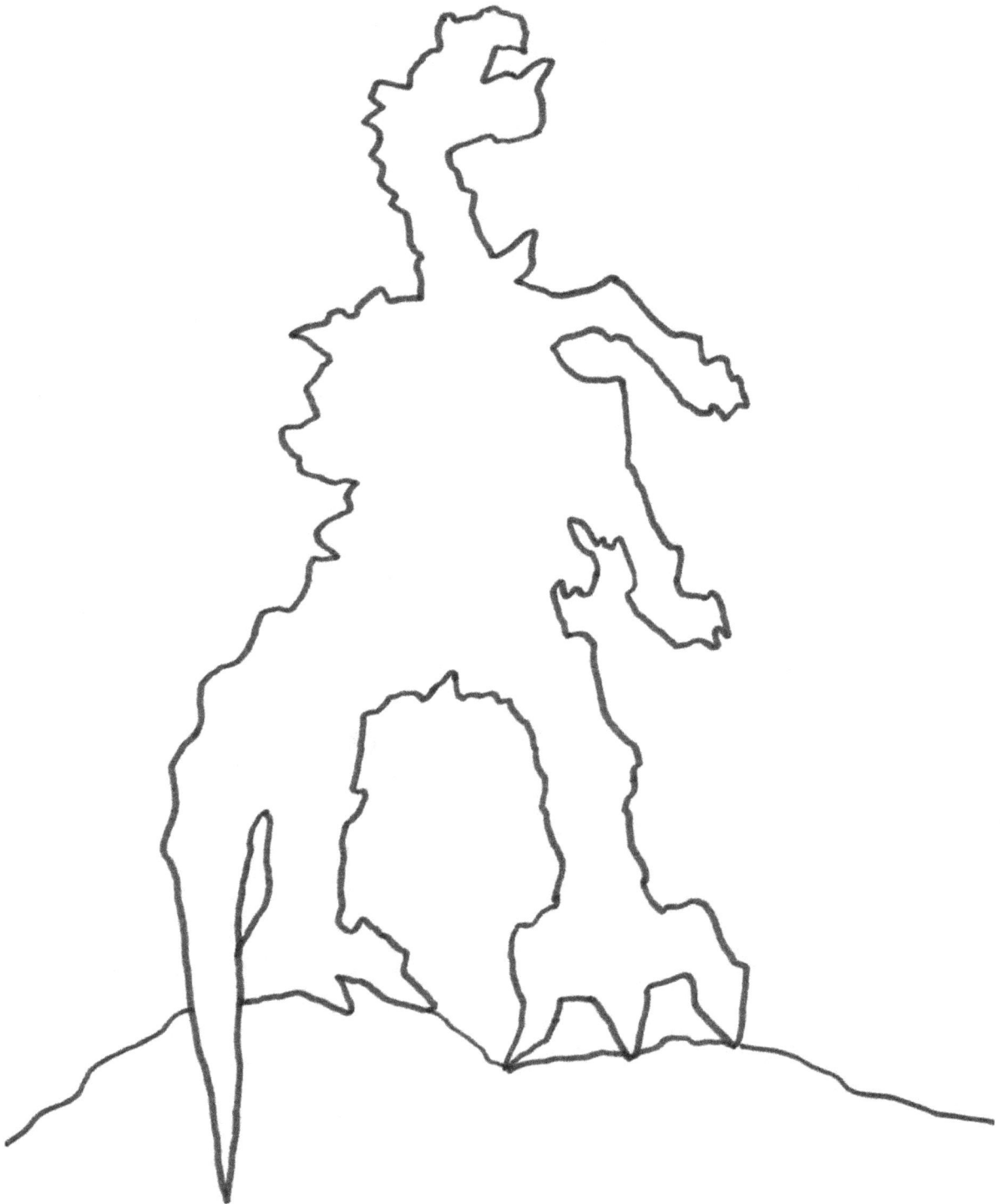

The Dragon of Krakow

Summary:

In a cave on the River Vistula lived a dragon who should never be disturbed. However some youths disturbed the dragon and it became very angry. A villager named Krakus managed to slay the dragon by baiting its food, making it drink until it exploded. Krakus was made leader of the prosperous city of Krakow.

Tale

The River Vistula has run for many centuries from the Tatra Mountains in southern Poland to the Baltic Sea at Gdansk. In its middle course is the city of Krakow and a local landmark: Wawel Hill.

There was a small village on the river near Wawel Hill. Near the village and behind an overgrown entrance lay a deep cave which many people believed to house a sleeping dragon. No-one dared go into the cave and no-one dared awaken the dragon otherwise bad things would happen to the villagers.

Youths can be short-sighted and let their curiosity get the better of them. A group of such youths went to explore the cave armed with nothing but torches. As you can probably guess, the clumsy youths awakened the sleeping dragon. They were face to face with fire, heavy breathing and anger. The dragon chased the boys out of the cave.

From that time on the dragon caused havoc in the village. It appeared from time to time and carried off sheep and young women. This became a real problem. How could the villagers be free from the dragon? What could they do?

One of the villagers, a wise shoe-maker named Krakus, had an idea. His plan was to bait the dragon's cave with sheep smeared in sulphur, a substance that would surely slay the dragon.

As luck would have it, the dragon ate the sheep and the sulphur created a terrible fire within him. To put out the fire it rushed to the river and started drinking. It drank and drank even more until finally there was a great explosion – yes, the dragon exploded!

The people of the village were happy again. Krakus was made leader of the village and soon a prosperous city grew around Wawel Hill: the city of Krakow.

Vocabulary:

Do you know these words? Look them up in your dictionary if you don't.

century – *one hundred years*
landmark – *a memorable place*
cave – *a hole in the mountain*
curiosity – *to want to know more*
torch – *a light to help you see*
havoc – *not in order, a mess*
idea – *something you think of*

plan – *something you will do*
explosion – *a big bang*
overgrown – *with a lot of plants and trees*
deep – *a lot of water, like the sea*
short-sighted – *can not see properly*
clumsy – *to move without thought*
wise – *to know a lot*
to believe – *to have faith*
to awaken – *to wake up*
to explore – *to go around and look at things*
to chase – *to run after*

Did you know?

❖ The 200ft 'Dragon's Cave' ('Smocza Jama') at Wawel Hill now attracts thousands of visitors each year.
❖ The River Vistula runs from the Tatra Mountains in Poland's deep south through Krakow, Warsaw and Torun, and enters the sea at Gdansk on Poland's Baltic Sea. Look at a map to find it.
❖ Dragons are a major motif in many cultures, for example the Turks who revere the 'sky dragon'.

What do you think?

1. Are dragons friendly or unfriendly?
2. Would you like to keep a dragon as a pet? Why?
3. Can dragons explode?
4. What do you think dragons eat?
5. What does a dragon look like?

Play: The Dragon of Krakow:

Characters

Dragon
Villagers
Old folk
Youths
Krakus
Narrator
(also: cave, Wawel Hill, Vistula River, sheep...)

Situation

We are in a small village, a long time ago, near the Vistula River and Wawel Hill. Birds sing gently in the trees, and the river ripples quietly by the village. Everyone is happy.

Script

Villager 1: We live in a beautiful village.
Villager 2: We have our homes and our family.
Villager 3: We are happy.
Narrator: On the other side of Wawel Hill is a spooky cave.
Youth 1: Let's go into the cave.
Old Folk 1: Don't go into the cave.
Old Folk 2: A dragon lives there.
Old Folk 3: Be careful. Bad things will happen.
Youths 2+3: That's rubbish. Don't listen. We're not scared.
Youth 1: Come on, the cave's this way.
Narrator: A thunderstorm gathered in the background. The stupid youths went to the spooky cave with torches.

Youth 1: Here's the cave. Let's go in. *(they walk in)*

Youth 2: What's that? *(dragon snores and wakes up)*

Dragon: Roar! I am a big angry dragon. I will eat you! Roar!

Youths 12&3: Wo-ah-ah! Run!

Narrator: The dragon chased the boys out of the cave.

Old Folk: Where have you been?

Youth 1: We went to the dragon's cave.

Old Folk: But we told you: an angry dragon lives there.

Youths 12&3: We know!!!

Narrator: Sometimes the dragon came to the village.

Dragon: I am hungry. I will eat your sheep.

Villagers 12&3: Oh no, it's the dragon! Run! Hide!

Krakus: Don't worry. I have an idea. The dragon likes to eat sheep. I will give him sheep with poison.

Narrator: He puts the sheep near the dragon's cave.

Dragon: Yummy! Sheep to eat!

Krakus: Look! The dragon is eating the sheep and poison.

Dragon: What? My tummy is on fire. I must drink water. Where is the river?

Narrator: The dragon drinks until it explodes. *(the dragon explodes)*

Old Folk: The dragon is gone.

Village Folk: Well done, Krakus, you saved us!

Narrator: The village grew into the city of Krakow. Birds sing gently in the trees, and the river ripples quietly by the city. Everyone is happy.

Villager 1: We live in a beautiful city.

Villager 2: We have our homes and our family.

Villager 3: We are happy.

Villagers 12&3: Hooray!

(All actors take a bow)

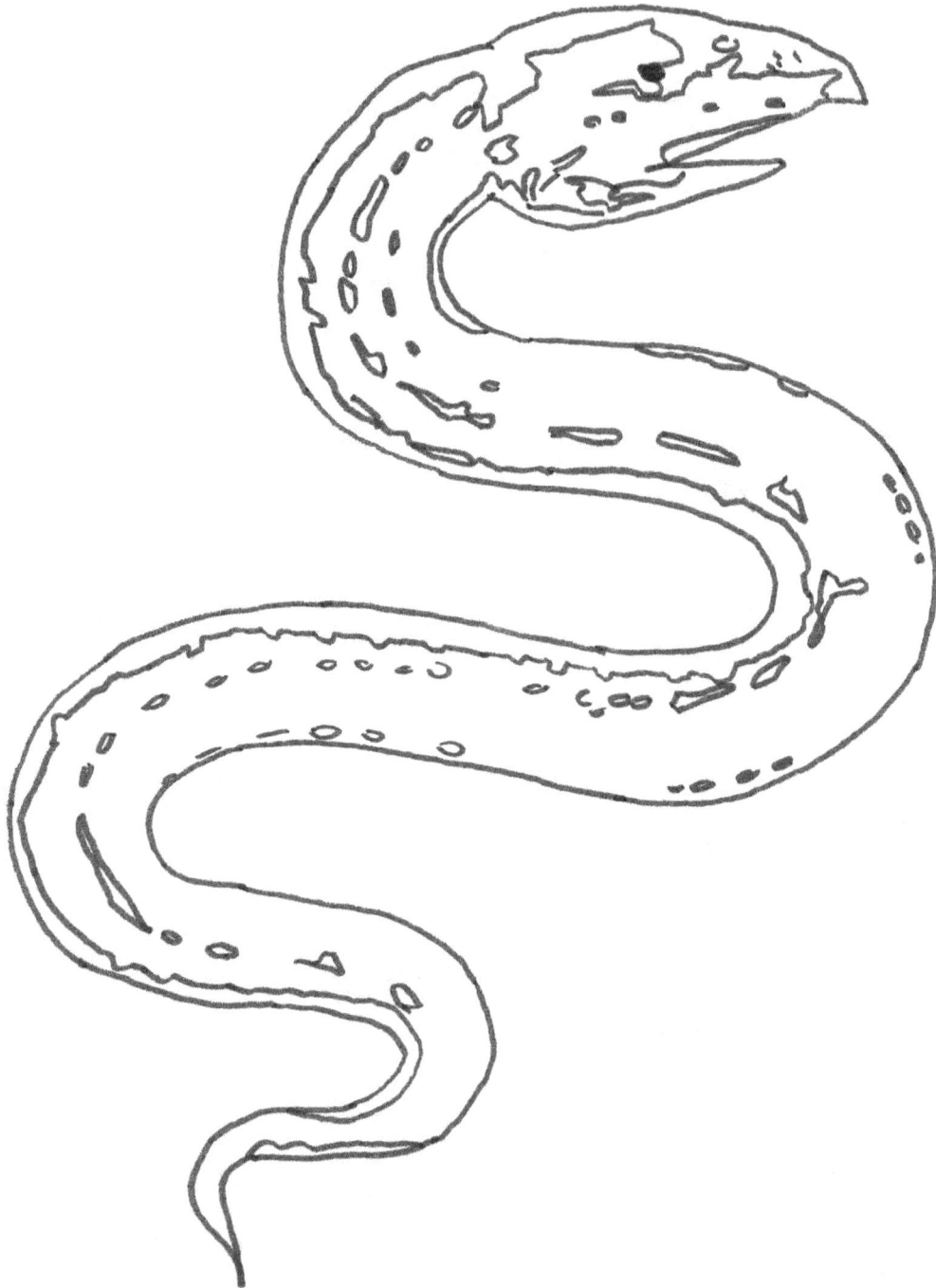

(2)

The Obra Water Monster

The Obra Water Monster

Summary

River Obra is home to a giant monster who attacks small animals and boats. But is it really just a giant catfish?

Tale

If you look at a map of modern-day Poland you will see in the west a blue line which is the River Warta. A small tributary of this is the River Obra, a remote and sparse area. These two rivers are home to a dinosaur-like water-loving monster similar to Nessie in Scotland.

It is snake-like in appearance as it serpents its way through the waters.

Many reliable witnesses have seen it.

What does the monster do? Apparently it attacks small animals such as ducks, swans and even small dogs. They are preyed upon and dragged under to their watery fate. The creature has even tried to upset small boats. It mainly hunts its prey at night.

So, is it really a monster? Some suggest that it is actually a giant European catfish, oversized. Similar giant catfish have attacked dogs and ducks in other locations in Europe. It has even been suggested that the Loch Ness Monster is, too, a giant catfish!

You can go there, and unless the tale of the Obra Water Monster frightens you, the area around the Rivers Warta and Obra are pleasant to visit.

Vocabulary

Do you know these words? Look them up in your dictionary if you don't.

catfish – *large fish whose face resembles a cat*
tributary – *a smaller river flowing into a bigger one*
remote and sparse area – *a place with nothing there*
serpent – *poisonous snake*
witness – *someone who has seen a special event or thing*
oversized – *bigger than normal*

Did you know?

- ❖ There are a lot of similar monsters around the world, for example the Mardin Dragon in Turkey or the infamous Loch Ness Monster in Scotland;
- ❖ All the water in Loch Ness is more than all the water in all the other lochs and lakes in Scotland and England;
- ❖ The River Obra is one of the longest rivers in Poland, and the longest is the Vistula which reaches the sea at Gdansk.

What do you think?

1. What does the Obra Water Monster look like?
2. What does it eat?
3. Why is the monster a problem?
4. Does the Obra Water Monster really exist?
5. Would you like to see the monster?

Play: The Obra Water Monster

Characters

Obra Water Monster
Witnesses – doctor, farmer, fisherman, boy, girl
Victims – duck, swan, duck

Setting

The banks of the River Obra, a remote area in Western Poland.

Script

Monster: Hello. I'm the Obra Water Monster. I'm hungry.
Duck: Quack. Oh no, it's the Obra Water Monster!
Monster: I'm hungry. I will eat you. *(chews)* Yummy!
Duck: Quack! Quack! Quack!
Fisherman: I don't believe it! Did you see that? The monster ate the duck!
Swan: *(glides in)* Oh no, it's the Obra Water Monster!
Monster: I'm hungry. I will eat you. *(chews)*. Yummy!
Swan: Flap! Flap! Flap!
Farmer: I don't believe it! Did you see that? The monster ate the swan!
Dog: Woof woof! Oh no, it's the Obra Water Monster!
Monster: I'm hungry. I will eat you. *(chews)* Yummy!
Dog: Woof! Woof! Woof!
Boy & Girl: We don't believe it! Did you see that? The monster ate the dog!
Monster: Hey fisherman! Hey farmer! Hey boy and girl!
Everyone: Yes?
Monster: I'm hungry.

Everyone: So?

Monster: I will eat you *(chases and chews wildly)* Yummy!

Narrator: I don't believe it! That's not in the script!

M: Oh shut up! I will eat you too!

(monster eats the narrator)

(All actors take a bow)

(3)

Rusalka: Tree-dwelling Spirit

Rusalka: Tree-dwelling Spirit

Summary

Rusalka is a type of dangerous tree-dwelling spirit whose power comes from her beauty. She lives near lakes and forests in sparse areas.

Tale

There is a type of tree-dwelling spirit that is the most dangerous of all. The name for this spirit is Rusalka (plural Rusalki). They can be found all over the Slavic world, and in Poland next to lakes and rivers in heavily forested areas. Some live in trees, others in rivers or lakes. In Poland this means the sparse areas of Western Pomerania and Lubuskie.

Legend says that this type of spirit is the most dangerous of all: they are girls or women who died an unnatural or violent death. Her power comes from her beauty and attractiveness, with her green eyes especially attractive to men. Her beauty and song is said to be enough to lure any man into the forest where they would be killed. Indeed, the spirit seeks to continue to exist by drawing the energy of life from all nearby living things.

Personally I wonder if this is a spirit, a ghost, or even an alien (after all it has green eyes). Aliens? That's another story.

Vocabulary

Do you know these words? Look them up in your dictionary if you don't.

tree-dwelling – *lives in and around trees*
violent – *with force*
to lure – *to attract*
alien – *a being from another planet*

Did you know?

❖ The plural of 'Rusalka' is 'Rusalki'. The fact that there may be more than one of these creatures makes the stomach churn!
❖ Western Pomerania and Lubuskie lie around Gdansk in northern Poland, and the area stretches towards the German border;
❖ The most common varieties of alien spaceship are discs, cigars, and shooting lights.

What do you think?

1. What do you think Rusalka looks like?
2. If you met her, what would you ask her?
3. What are the most 'sparse and remote' areas of your country?
4. Do aliens ("little green men") exist?
5. Have you ever seen an alien?

Play: Rusalka: Tree-dwelling Spirit

Characters

Rusalka
Man
Birds
Small Animals
Trees
Lake

Setting

A dark forest in Poland. Here and there are small lakes. There are no flowers, but many birds and small animals. A man walks alone in the forest.

Script

Man: What a beautiful forest. Look at the birds.
Birds: Cheep! Cheep! Hello.
Man: Look at the small animals.
Small Animals: *(various small animal noises)* Hello.
Man: Look at the trees.
Trees: *(wave their leaves and branches)* Hello.
Man: Look at the lake.
Lake: *(waves and ripples)* Hello.
Man: It's a beautiful place.
(Later...)
Rusalka: I am Rusalka. I am not good. I am bad. *(she looks around. She sees the man)* Who is this? (she jumps out)
Man: Oh, hello. I, I, I... love you!

Birds: Don't look in her eyes!

Small Animals: Don't look in her eyes!

Trees: Don't look in her eyes!

Lake: Don't look in her eyes!

(A little later...)

Man: You have beautiful eyes.

Rusalka: Yes, and I will eat you!

(she grabs the man and eats him)

Birds: Oh, no.

Small Animals: He didn't listen.

Trees: Be careful in the dark forest.

(All actors take a bow)

(4)

The Mermaid of Warsaw

The Mermaid of Warsaw

Summary

While a prince was hunting he came across a mermaid who directed him to a cottage in a clearing. He met a young woman who had twin babies. He gave the land to her and told her to plant crops – thus starting the city of Warsaw.

Tale

Syrenka is a freshwater mermaid who has become the symbol of Warsaw. First known as a royal seal dated 1390, the figure has evolved over the years into a mermaid form, with great beauty ("film star looks" as inyourpocket.com puts it).

A prince from the Mazowsze region took his men hunting in the forest. He saw a wild beast and was determined to take it home, but as he took his aim it suddenly disappeared. He was very surprised, but decided to stop off at the river for a drink. As he cupped his hands to drink, he saw a mermaid. She shot an arrow from her bow and told him to follow it.

Eventually he reached a clearing. In the middle was an old fisherman's cottage and a large oak tree. He entered the cottage. Inside was a young woman and her two twin babies: one boy and one girl. They were sitting by the fireplace. The young woman shared her food with the prince, and then they went outside to look at the river. As the woman listened to the prince she saw the mermaid rise from the ripples of the river. The mermaid said that the village would grow into a beautiful city.

In conversation, the prince insisted that the twins be named Wars and Sawa. He gave the land surrounding the cottage to the woman, and told her to plant crops. So she did.

He knew they would work hard and, indeed, this was the start of today's Warsaw, the capital of Poland.

Vocabulary

Do you know these words? Look them up in your dictionary if you don't.

mermaid – *half woman, half fish*
fresh water – *non-salty water found in rivers (not in the sea)*
(royal) seal – *royal coat of arms, or symbol of the royal family*
beast – *wild animal*
clearing – *a place with no trees in the middle of the forest*
twins – *two children born at the same time*
crops – *things farmers grow to sell, eg. wheat, corn or apples*

Did you know?

❖ A mermaid is a mythical creature. The top half is a beautiful woman or girl, the bottom half a fishes tail;
❖ There is a male version called a 'merboy', and the cat version is a 'mercat';
❖ Campsites are often located in clearings in the middle of a forest, and they are the polar opposite to an oasis in a desert.

What do you think?

1. What is your mind's image of a mermaid?
2. Where do mermaids live? In a cave?
3. Do you know any twins?
4. Do they look alike?
5. Were they born at the same time?

Play: The Mermaid of Warsaw

Characters

The Prince
Young woman
The Mermaid (Syrenka)
Huntsmen 1 & 2
The two twins (one boy, one girl)
Deer
Narrator
(Also: river, forest, cottage, crops, city / people…)

Setting

A forest in Central Poland, dark and a little spooky. Wild deer wander at ease, and the river gently flows.

Script

Syrenka: Hello. My name's Syrenka and I'm a freshwater mermaid. I am helpful. I will help the prince. I can help you, too!
Prince: Come on, men. Let's find a deer!
Huntsman 1: This way!

Huntsman 2: This way!

Prince: No... this way!

Narrator: They walk into the dark forest.

Prince: Look – a deer. I want to kill it. I want to eat it.

Deer: Oh, no! I'm off! *(the deer runs off quickly)*

Huntsman 1: Where's the deer?

Huntsman 2: It ran away.

Prince: Never mind, I'm thirsty. *(they go to the river bank and drink)*

Syrenka: Hello, Prince. Follow my arrow. *(she shoots her arrow).*

Prince: Men, I will see you later.

Huntsmen 1&2: Where are you going?

Prince: I need to follow the mermaid's arrow.

Huntsmen 1&2: What? You're crazy. See you later!

(the prince follows the mermaid's arrow to a small clearing. He sees a cottage and goes inside)

Young Woman: Hello. Who are you?

Prince: I am a prince. How are you?

Young Woman: Fine, thank you.

Prince: And you babies?

Babies: We're fine, thank you. Waaahh! *(they sit and look at the river)*

Syrenka: You are good people. Start a village and it will grow into a strong and beautiful city.

Prince: Yes, with your two baby twins, Wars and Sawa.

Babies: Wars and Sawa? *(they think)* Hmm, good names. Waaahh!

Narrator: And so the city of Warsaw began.

(All actors take a bow)

Part 2

Kings, Queens and Royalty

(5)

King Boleslaw and his Knights

King Boleslaw and his Knights

Summary

Boleslaw and his Knights supposedly lie in waiting in a cave in the Tatra Mountains should Poland ever need them. The tale is similar to the story 'The Sleeping Knights' (Chapter 8).

Tale

King Boleslaw (a Polish version of King Arthur) was a brave and popular ruler, who united Poland and made it into a great country. Apparently they earned the title 'brave' because they defeated Poland's enemies.

There is a mountain called Giewont in the Tatra Mountains and its shape, seen from a certain angle, resembles the head of a sleeping knight. It is said that within the mountain is a huge dark cavern and within this cavern sleep King Boleslaw and his Knights who are mounted on horses with their swords, bows and arrows and lances beside them, and it is said that if Poland ever needed them, they will awaken and ride forth to serve Poland.

There is one caveat: once they have gone forth, they will never return, apparently.

These days there are rumours going round of a steam train packed full of gold under these mountains – but that's another story!

Vocabulary

Do you know these words? Look them up in your dictionary if you don't.

knight – *one of the King's soldiers*
brave – *without fear*
swords, bows, arrows and lances – *weapons of fighting and war*
caveat – *a condition set for something to happen*
to go forth – *to emerge, to come out, usually quickly*

Did you know?

- ❖ In Britain there are 'Knights' (men) and 'Dames' (women);
- ❖ In order to be knighted in Britain, you must kneel before the King or Queen;
- ❖ The 'Four Knights' of British popular music are Sir Paul McCartney, Sir Elton John, Sir Cliff Richard, and Sir Tom Jones.

What do you think?

1. What do King Boleslaw and his Knights look like? Can you try to draw them?
2. Can you play "I-Spy"?
3. What games do you like to play? Tell me.
4. Do you know any similar stories?
5. How often do you 'play fight' with your friends?

Play: King Boleslaw and His Knights

Characters

King Boleslaw
Knight 1
Knight 2
Knight 3
Stallions 12&3

Setting

A dark cavern, deep underground. King Boleslaw and His Knights are chatting.

Script

Boleslaw: So, men, here we are again.
Knight 1: Another day when nothing happens.
Knight 2: Yes, sometimes it's so boring.
Knight 3: What can we do today?
Boleslaw: Let's play a game. *(he thinks)* How about "I-Spy"?
Knights 1,2 and 3: Hmmmm, OK.
Boleslaw: I'll start. I spy with my little eye something beginning with "R".
Knight 1: Rock.
Boleslaw: Correct! Well done! Now it's your turn.
Knight 1: I spy with my little eye something beginning with "H".
Knight 2: Horse.
Knight 1: Correct! Now it's your turn.
Knight 2: I spy with my little eye something beginning with "S".
Knight 3: Sword?

Knight 2: No. Try again.
Knight 1: Stone?
Knight 2: No. Try again.
Boleslaw: Stallion?
Knight 2: No. Try again.
Boleslaw: We give up. What is it?
Knight 2: Snake! Run!!!
Everyone: Ahhhhhhhhhh!!! *(they all run)*

(All actors take a bow)

(6)

The Queen of the Baltic

The Queen of the Baltic

Summary

Jurata, the Queen of the Baltic, had a palace made of amber at the bottom of the sea. She loved fish, but decided to punish a fisherman. But when she saw how handsome she was she declared her love for him. A jealous God destroyed her palace and the Queen of the Baltic and her lover both died.

Tale

Can you imagine an incredible palace made from amber at the bottom of the ocean? There once was such a palace at the bottom of the Baltic which belonged to Jurata, Queen of the Baltic.

Jurata was a wise and caring Queen, and looked after her people well. She was very fond of animals. For example, when her favourite fish, flounders, was served, only half was eaten and the other half thrown back into the sea.

Can you imagine her outrage when she saw a fisherman casting his net into the river? She decided to punish the fisherman. She enticed him onto her amber boat to carry out the punishment. But when she saw the young man he was so handsome that instead of punishing him she declared her love for him.

Every evening she swam to the river shore to see her lover.

Some people can be angry or jealous, and even Gods can be angry or jealous. Piorun, the God of Thunder, was angry and jealous. He created a big storm and threw down thunderbolts destroying the Queen's amber palace at the bottom of the ocean. The calamity killed the Queen and her lover, the fisherman. He was chained to the bottom... of the sea!

To this day when there is a storm, his laments can be heard. And the amber that washes ashore on the Baltic are fragments of Jurata's amber palace and boat, apparently.

Vocabulary

Do you know these words? Look them up in your dictionary if you don't.

amber, jade – *precious stones*
punishment – *a penalty when you have done something wrong*
handsome – *beautiful and sexy man*
jealous – *to envy or wish one had someone's possessions*
thunderbolts – *lightning, in a storm*
calamity – *disaster*
laments – *sad songs or chants*
fragments – *bits and pieces, parts*

Did you know?

- ❖ The main Polish city on the Baltic Sea is Gdansk;
- ❖ Poland's neighbours on the Baltic are Germany to the west and Russia to the east;
- ❖ The mighty Malbork Castle, thirty kilometres southeast of Gdansk, is Europe's largest Gothic castle and was seat to the Teutonic Knights.

What do you think?

1. What do you think of vegetarians?
2. Should we eat meat or fish?
3. Don't vegetables have rights, too?
4. What's the nearest castle to your school or office?
5. Why were castles built?

Play: Queen of the Baltic: Love at First Sight

Characters

Jurata, Queen of the Baltic
Fisherman
Piorun, God of Thunder
Fish

Setting

The mouth of a river on the Baltic Coast. Small villages and sand dunes. A great amber palace lies beneath the water.

Script

Jurata: I am Jurata, Queen of the Baltic! Welcome to my undersea palace made of amber! Isn't it beautiful? *(she signals to the amber palace).*
Fish: Hello. I am a fish. She loves her animals. She loves her people. She is a good queen.
Jurata: Hello, fish. How are you? Don't worry, I won't eat you.
Fish: Thank you, Queen of the Baltic.
Jurata: What's that? Someone is fishing! I am angry. I must kill him!
(she gets into her amber boat)

Fisherman: *(sings hapilly)* lalalalala...

Jurata: *(she shouts)* Hey, you! *(she pauses)*... beautiful man! I love you!

Fisherman: Queen of the Baltic! I love you, too.

(they kiss, but suddenly...)

Piorun: Roar! You can't do that! *(he throws lightning at the couple)* Roar!

Jurata: Oh, no, I'm dead!

Fisherman: Oh, no, I'm dead too!

Piorun: Hahaha!

Narrator: To this day you can hear Pioran's roar, Jurata's cries, and the young fisherman's lament on the Baltic Coast of Poland.

(All actors take a bow)

(7)

The Legend of Wanda

The Legend of Wanda

Summary

Wanda was a wise and good Queen and led a proud Poland. A German Prince, Rytigier, tried to blackmail her into marrying him but instead of giving in she drowned herself in the River Vistula.

Tale

Wanda was a beautiful lady, but she was a young girl when she became Queen. She ruled wisely and her people showed her love and respect: she had a wisdom and understanding beyond her years. She herself led her soldiers into the battlefield, and she led them to victory.

Because of her beauty and wisdom, she was approached by many princes wanting to marry her. But she found none of them pleasing or able to help her rule wisely.

There was a problem – a German prince, Rytigier, had designs on Wanda. He had heard of her beauty, and that Poland was "fruitful and rich" (anglik.net). His messengers were looked after with courtesy, even though they seemed rough and uncivilised. They seemed surprised at the luxury and comfort of Wanda's palace, and looked around respectfully but with an air of greed.

Wanda did not like the letter that the messengers had brought. Rytigier asked for her hand in marriage and, if not, threatened to invade and take over Poland. Rytigier had a very strong army and would surely win, but to accept his proposal of marriage was unthinkable.

What could she do? How could she wage war against such a strong army? She refused firmly.

She retired to her apartment and prayed to God to grant Poland freedom from the Germans in exchange for her life. Her prayer was granted, and she threw herself in the River Vistula. They found her body, and she was buried with full honours beside her father, Krakus.

Vocabulary

Do you know these words? Look them up in your dictionary if you don't.

wisdom – *cleverness, and understanding of the world*
victory – *success*
to have designs on someone – *to fancy someone*
courtesy – *politeness*
rough and uncivilized – *noisy and uneducated*
luxurious – *comfortable, worth a lot of money*
to refuse – *to say "no"*
full honours – *to give with the greatest respect and humbleness*

Did you know?

- ❖ Germany shares Poland's western land border;
- ❖ Other neighbouring countries with land borders are the Czech Republic, Slovakia, Ukraine, Belarus, and Russia;
- ❖ Krakus gives his name to modern-day Krakow.

What do you think?

1. Was Wanda right to refuse Rytigier's offer?
2. What would you have done?
3. Do you know any wise people? Who?
4. Do you know any 'rough and uncivilised' people? Who?
5. What is the most luxurious hotel in your area?

Play: The Legend of Wanda

Characters

Queen Wanda
Person 1
Person 2
Prince Rytigier
Messenger 1
Messenger 2
God

Setting

A fine and comfortable palace.

Script

Queen Wanda: Hello. My name is Queen Wanda. I am a good Queen.
Person 1: We love you, Queen Wanda.
Person 2: You are a good Queen.
Queen Wanda: Thank you.
(pause)

Rytigier: What's this? A beautiful Queen with a lot of money and a fine comfortable palace? I will marry her.

(pause)

Queen Wanda: Welcome, guests. Sit down, please.

Messenger 1: Thank you, Queen Wanda.

Queen Wanda: What is this?

Messenger 2: We have a message from Prince Rytigier.

Queen Wanda: Give it to me.

Messengers 1&2: Here you are.

(she reads the message in her head:)

Queen Wanda: "Marry me. You must marry me. Or I will take away your palace and your country".

Persons 1&2: What does it say?

Queen Wanda: It says I must marry Prince Rytigier or he will take my palace and our country. I hate Prince Rytigier!

Person 1: Oh, no! What will you do?

Queen Wanda: I will pray. *(she kneels and prays)* Oh, God, what shall I do?

God: Hmm, let me think... go and throw yourself in the river!

Queen Wanda: OK, I'll do it. *(she throws herself in the river)* Ahhhhh! I'm dead!

Person 1: Our Queen is dead.

Person 2: But now the evil Prince Rytigier won't take her palace or our country.

God: Until he tries again...

(All actors take a bow)

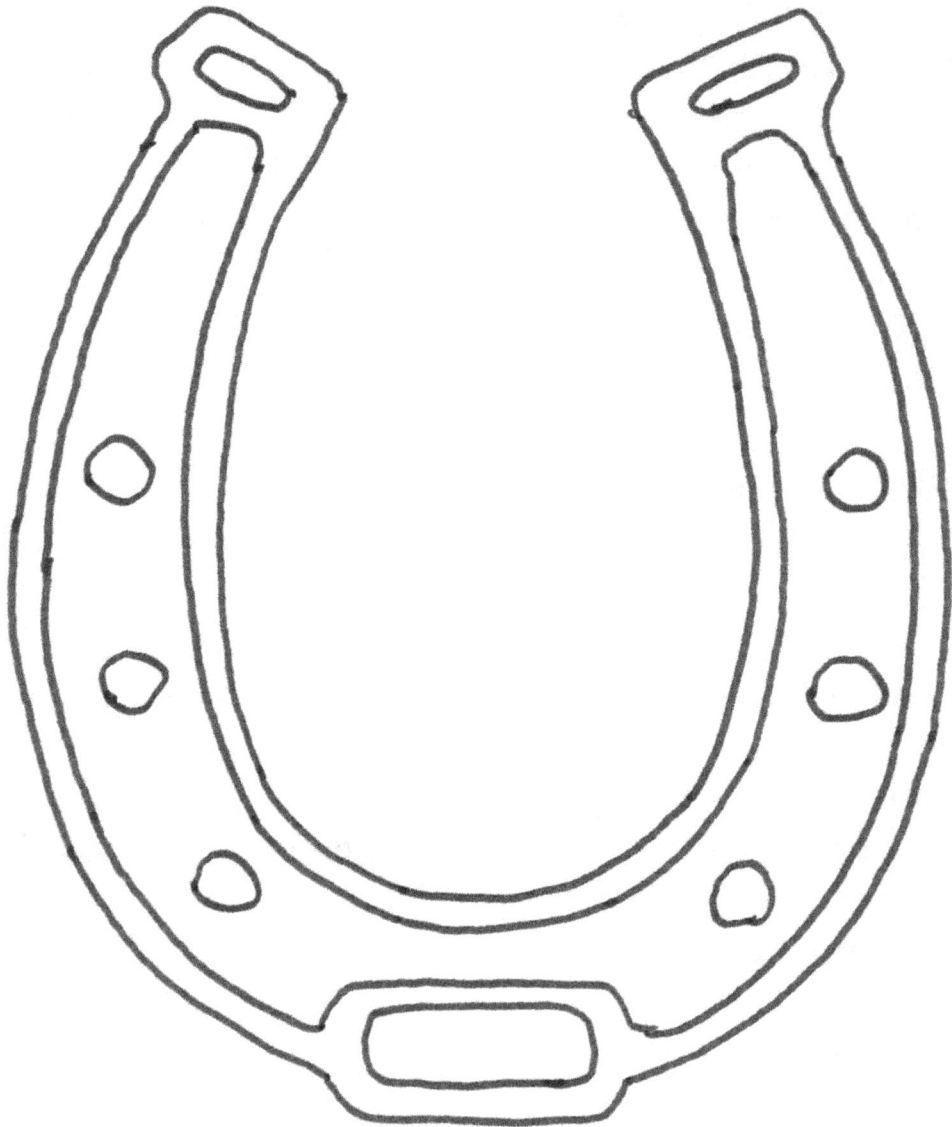

(8)

The Sleeping Knights

The Sleeping Knights

Summary

A stranger asked the village blacksmith to make a golden horseshoe, and led him to a cave to fit the shoe. Inside there was an army of sleeping knights and horses who would only wake in a time of trouble. The tale claims that the bravest knights never die, but are asleep in this cave beneath Mount Pisana.

Tale

Long ago there was a quiet mountain village. A stranger went into the blacksmith's shop and asked him to make a special horseshoe – of gold. The blacksmith could earn a rich reward but he couldn't tell anyone. The blacksmith agreed.

The stranger took a gold bar from under his coat and the blacksmith duly made a golden horseshoe. The stranger led the blacksmith to the Koscieliska Valley and finally, after hours of walking, they came to a cave hidden by rocks and trees.

Inside the cave was a bright golden light, and a sight the blacksmith couldn't believe: an army of knights in full armour, resting their heads upon saddles like pillows. Along the walls stood beautiful sleeping horses, all wearing horseshoes made of gold.

The blacksmith duly replaced a broken shoe on one of the stallions. As he nailed the shoe to the stallion's hoof, it made no movement.

The stranger would only say that the knights had been in deep sleep for hundreds of years, and would not wake up until time came for a big battle. On that day, thunder would shake the earth, giant pine trees would break like little sticks, and boulders would crash down the mountainsides. The knights would then wake up to defend Poland one more time.

When the blacksmith was finished, the stranger led him back to the village. He was made to swear that he would tell no-one. The stranger paid with a bag of gold and then vanished.

You can guess what happened next, can't you? Yes, the blacksmith told his wife, then his neighbours, and soon everyone knew the secret. His bag of gold turned to sand, and try as he might, he was never able to find the cave again.

Vocabulary

Do you know these words? Look them up in your dictionary if you don't.

blacksmith – *someone who makes things from metal*
reward – *something given for good work or duty*
stranger – *an unknown person*
armour – *metal clothes worn by knights and soldiers*
saddle – *a seat you put on a horse*
battle – *fight, war*
to swear – *to promise, to give one's word*
to vanish – *to disappear*
neighbours – *people who live near you*
secret – *something you shouldn't tell anyone*
to try as you might – *to try very hard, again and again*

Did you know?

- ❖ Mount Pisana, where the story takes place, is located in the Beskid / Tatra Mountains in the deep south of the country;
- ❖ The largest and most developed ski resort in the area is Zakopane, but others include Nowy Targ, Krynica, Stary Sacz, and Szczyrk.
- ❖ In winter the area is popular for skiing and snowboarding; in summer it is especially good for walking and hiking. Take a hearty picnic and lots of water!

What do you think?

1. Have you heard this story before?
2. How many hours do you sleep every day?
3. What time do you go to bed?
4. What time do you get up?
5. What does a blacksmith do?

Play: The Sleeping Knights

Characters

A stranger
A blacksmith

Setting

Wooded valleys and low mountains in Poland. A river with some flowers, birds, and small animals. There is a small village.

Script

Blacksmith: Oh, it's a hard life. All day long I have to hammer my metal into place. Bang! Bang! Bang! Hammer, hammer, hammer!
Stranger: Hello, blacksmith.
Blacksmith: Hello, stranger. How are you?
Stranger: I'm fine, thanks. And you?
Blacksmith: I'm fine, too. How can I help you?
Stranger: I wonder if you could help me. I need a golden horseshoe. Can you help me?
Blacksmith: Yes, I can help you. *(they walk to a dark cave in the mountains)*
Stranger: Here is a dark cave. Let's go inside. *(they go inside)*
Blacksmith: Wow! It's amazing! Look at all those knights and horses! What are they doing?
Stranger: They are sleeping.
Blacksmith: OK, how can I help you?
Stranger: Please put a new golden shoe on this horse.
Blacksmith: OK. *(he nails the golden horseshoe to the stallion's hoof)*
Stranger: Thank you. Here is your bag of gold.
Blacksmith: Oh, thank you very much. Goodbye.
Stranger: Goodbye.

(All actors take a bow)

Part 3

Common People

(9)

Janosik:
Polish Robin Hood

Janosik: Polish Robin Hood

Summary

Janosik is the closest Poland has to Robin Hood; he robbed from the rich and gave to the poor. A major difference is that he had magical powers. He and his men lived in the Tara Mountains on both the Polish and Slovak sides.

Tale

Janosik and his men hid out in the foothills of the Tatra Mountains, on both the Polish and Slovak sides. He became a local hero for his benevolent attitude towards the poor, he was a robber and with his group of friends he robbed the manor houses of the rich. He gave his pickings to the poor.

He was well known for his magical powers which three witches had given him when he was young. Seeing his courageous character they decided to make him the most famous robber in all history and gave him three magic objects: an alpenstok (shepherd's stick), a magic shirt, and a magic belt.

What about his magical powers? It was said that he had a magical resistance to arrows, bullets and wounds by use of a special herb which he carried in his side pocket. He also had the ability to move from one place to another quicker than any other human being; and the extraordinary ability to leave the impression of his palm in solid rock. How could he do that?

Though he was able to evade all traps and enemies, he was eventually betrayed by a girlfriend. She carefully destroyed the three gifts that the witches had given him. So, Janosik was unable to defend himself and was captured by the King's soldiers. Of course, the young lady was well rewarded!

Janosik has been the subject of much media, both TV and film. Janosik (1935) is a black and white Slovak film; Janosik I and II (1962/3) are similarly Slovak action films; Janosik (1974) is a Polish film; and finally Janosik (1975) has been a long-running Polish TV series. I have not seen any of these, but I am sure they are very good when viewed in conjunction with a translation device.

Vocabulary

Do you know these words? Look them up in your dictionary if you don't.

foothills – *small hills near the base of a mountain*
benevolent – *kind and generous, especially to the poor*
manor houses – *houses of the rich and gentry*
shepherd – *someone who watches over sheep*
to betray – *to trick, to break one's trust*

Did you know?

❖ Did you know you can watch "Janosik" on the internet?
❖ Robin Hood Airport Doncaster Sheffield operated its first passenger flight in 2005, to Palma de Mallorca;
❖ Long haul flights to North America began in 2007.

What do you think?

1. Was Janosik a good man or a bad man?
2. What three questions would you ask him?
3. What does Janosik look like?
4. Would you like his magical powers?
5. Look at your classmates and friends. Who is Janosik?

Play: Janosik: Polish Robin Hood

Characters

Janosik
King
King's soldiers
Janosik's girlfriend

Setting

A forest in the Tatra Mountains. There is a small poor village and, above, a castle on a high rock.

Script

(a loud bang)
Janosik: HaHa! I am Janosik. I am magic. I steal from the rich and give to the poor. Look at me! *(he points at his magnificent clothes)*
(Later...)
King: I am not happy. I am angry. That bad Janosik must be stopped.
King's Soldiers: *(altogether)* Why, King?
King: Because he stole my money! He stole my clothes! Now he wants to steal my crown!

King's Soldiers: *(altogether)* Oh, no! What can we do?

King: We must stop him. Now! *(bangs fist on table)*

(Later…)

Janosik: HaHa! Me again! Look at my magic powers! HaHa! I can put my hand into solid rock *(puts hand in rock)*. HaHa! You can fire an arrow at me and I am still alive *(one of Janosik's men shoots an arrow at him)*

King: Stop! We must kill you!

Janosik: HaHa! No way! I'm off! *(he runs away quickly)*

King's Soldier # 1: How can we catch him?

King's Soldier # 2: He is too fast.

Janosik's Girlfriend: I can help you. Give me gold and I will help you.

King's Soldiers: Here you are. *(they give her gold)*

(Later…)

Janosik's Girlfriend: Oh, darling, I love you.

Janosik: HaHa! I love you too.

King's Soldiers: *(they run in)* HaHa! We've caught you! *(they take him away)*

Janosik's Girlfriend: Look at my gold. Look at my beautiful gold! *(she waves the gold in the air)*

(All actors take a bow)

(10)

The Trumpeter Of Krakow

The Trumpeter of Krakow

Summary

Krakow was threatened with an invasion, so the trumpeter played a tune over and over to warn the city. However, one arrow hit him and he died. To honour this sacrifice, the tune is played hourly even to this day.

Tale

If you go to Krakow these days you can hear a trumpet played from the second highest tower of St Mary's Church in the main square. In fact it is a bugle (military trumpet) but here I will call it a trumpet. It is the tune, or fanfare, that is most interesting. It is a fair tune, but ends suddenly. Why does it end so abruptly? Let's find out...

In the old days things were not as safe as they are now, and life was difficult. The people of Krakow knew this well. Though they had a good life, they were always threatened by invasion. Who wanted to invade Krakow? Their enemies, the Tatars. Why were the Tartars so feared? Because they stole money and gold, and killed many of the good people of Krakow. In fact, nobody liked them.

One day, a watchman on one of the highest towers saw the Tartar army getting closer. He knew they were going to invade – but what could he do? How could he warn the people of Krakow?

He decided to get his old trumpet and play the song 'hejnal' over and over again ('hejnal' means 'Hymn to our Lady').

Indeed, the people of Krakow heard and understood the warning. They prepared for battle. Everyone was involved: the soldiers, the archers, the landlords and the workers. All the women and children were kept safe.

Many arrows flew.

One of the arrows hit the watchman as he played his trumpet. The tune stopped suddenly.

After the Tartars had gone away, the people found the old watchman at the top of the tower. A single arrow had killed him, but Krakow was saved.

To honour his sacrifice, the city people decided to play the tune, hejnal, every day. And if you go to Krakow today, you can still hear the 'broken tune' of the hejnal echo above the ancient rooftops. It is played four times, once in each direction (north, south, east and west) and it always ends on the 'broken' note.

It is easy to find St Mary's Church as it is located in the main (market) square. It is the one with towers of two sizes (the lower one is where the trumpeter stood). Built of pinkish stone in the Gothic style, it has a fancy interior. You can visit the Church and even climb the tower. The view is amazing, apparently.

Vocabulary

Do you know these words? Look them up in your dictionary if you don't.

main square – *paved area in the centre of town, often with a market*
bugle – *military trumpet*
fanfare – *simple tune played on a trumpet*
abruptly – *suddenly*
watchman – *a security man, often on a high tower*
hymn – *religious song*
archer – *someone who uses a bow and arrow*
landlord – *owner of property or land*

Did you know?

❖ St. Mary's Church in Krakow has two towers, and it is the shorter of the two where the trumpeter stood all those years ago;
❖ The square in Krakow is the largest square in Europe;
❖ A Christmas Market is held in the square every December. Come and buy your presents!

What do you think?

1. In the old days a trumpet was the best way to warn of danger. How can we warn of danger these days?
2. Does your school or office have a fire alarm? What does it sound like?
3. Can you play a musical instrument?
4. What are your favourite songs?
5. Do you like karaoke?

Play: The Trumpeter of Krakow

Characters

The Trumpeter
Market Trader 1
Market Trader 2
Children (unspoken part)
Invaders (The Tartar Army)

Setting

The old city of Krakow, many years ago: red-tiled rooftops and church spires. People are busy in the market square.

Script

Trumpeter: I love to play the trumpet from the tower of St. Mary's Church. Listen. Toot-too-toot-too-toot.
Market Trader 1: The trumpet is like a clock. We can tell the time.
Market Trader 2: The trumpet can also warn us of danger. It is like an alarm.
Trumpeter: Why do we need an alarm? Because there are some bad people, the Tatars, near our town.
Market Trader 1: They want to fight us and kill us.
Market Trader 2: They want to take our money.
Trumpeter: We have to be careful.
(one day, the Tatar invaders appear)
Invaders: Forward! Charge! Destroy the town! Take the money!
Trumpeter: I will play my trumpet. It is an alarm. Toot-too-toot-too-toot.

Invaders: What? Look at the church tower. There is a man playing a trumpet. We must stop him.

Market Trader 1: What? He is playing his trumpet at a strange time.

Market Trader 2: Yes. We must be in danger. Let's go inside quickly. Come along, children!

Invaders: Shoot an arrow at the tower. We must kill the trumpeter! *(an arrow is shot; it hits the trumpeter)*

Trumpeter: Oh, no! I am hit! Toot-too-toot-too--- *(suddenly stops)*.

(the market traders fight the invaders and win)

Market Trader 1: We won! Hooray!

Market Trader 2: Yes. But what about the trumpeter?

Trumpeter: I am hit Ughhhhhh!!!!!! *(he dies)*.

Market Trader 1: We will always remember the Trumpeter of Krakow.

Market Trader 2: He saved us.

(All actors take a bow)

(11)

The
Three
Brothers

The Three Brothers

Summary

Three brothers, Lech, Czech and Rus, inherited both land and wealth, but their lands were overpopulated. So, they set off together, and then in their own three directions, to found lands of their own. Lech stayed in the land that is now modern-day Poland.

Tale

Imagine the low-lying lands at the mouth of the River Vistula, with fertile and well-irrigated fields and farmsteads. Now imagine this scene in early medieval times. There lived a wealthy King who had three sons, Lech, Czech and Rus. Following the King's death his land and possessions was divided between them and, because the Kingdom was very small, the three brothers decided to go in search of new lands. Lech was the eldest brother, and so it was naturally decided that he should lead and make the final decisions.

The three travelled for months through forests and wild country but finally came upon green hills in the midst of a fertile land. On top of the largest hill stood a grand old oak tree, above which flew a majestic white eagle. The eagle flew in great swooping circles and the three stood in awe at the beautiful sight. To top it off, as the sun set with a full surround of red, the eagle appeared pure white, with its wings tipped with gold.

Lech declared that the white eagle was a sign from the Gods, and said he would climb the tree to better observe the surroundings. As he climbed he saw the eagle's nest high in the branches, and though he could not get close to the nest, he could see long distances in every direction. To the north he saw lots of water. To the south he saw hills and mountains. To the east he saw flat and fertile land. And to the west he saw thick, dark forest.

Czech decided to go south; Rus decided to go east; and Lech declared that the best place was right where they were. Most people agreed with Lech and stayed to build a town on the hill. So, Lech became the first Duke of Poland and the town became the capital of Poland.

Though none of the sources specify, I take this "new" town to be Krakow, and the "hill" to be Wawel Hill.

Vocabulary

Do you know these words? Look them up in your dictionary if you don't.

fertile fields – *land with lots of goodness and nutrients*
irrigation – *a system of getting water around fields*
majestic – *like royalty, grand*
to swoop – *to fly free, like a bird*
capital city – *the biggest city*

Did you Know?

- ❖ The three brothers, Lech, Czech and Rus, correspond to the three modern-day lands of Poland, the Czech Republic / Slovakia, and Russia / Belarus;
- ❖ You can see the original hill in Krakow (Wawel Hill);
- ❖ The author has one elder brother.

What do you think?

1. Which of the three brothers would you follow? Why?
2. Have you ever seen an eagle? Where?
3. What are the most famous birds in your country?
4. Do you prefer the city or the country? Why?
5. If you could make your own country, what would it be like?

Play: The Three Brothers

Characters

Lech
Czech
Rus
King
Eagle
Common People

Setting

Lowlands near Krakow, with one large hill with an oak tree and eagle's nest

Script

Scene 1 (countryside)

(Lech, Czech and Rus slap hands together, musketeer style)
Lech, Czech and Rus: Yo!
Lech: Hey bro!
Czech: Hey bro!

Rus: Hey bro!

Lech: Hello, we are Lech, Czech and Rus, the three brothers.

Czech: We are not only brothers, but also good friends.

Rus: And we have a story to tell.

(Lech, Czech and Rus slap hands together again, musketeer style)

Lech, Czech and Rus: Yo!

Scene 2 (Royal Palace)

King: Oh, my children, my sons, I am dying. My life was long and happy. Please, my children, make sure you have a long and happy life.

Lech: Oh, father, we will miss you so much.

Czech: Yes, we will often think of you.

Rus: And we will never forget you.

King: Oh, my sons, I love you. Goodbye. *(the King dies)*

Scene 3 (in the countryside)

Lech: Brothers, let us go forth and seek new lands.

Czech: Let us find new adventures.

Rus: And boldly go where we have not been before.

Lech: Yes, our father would have wanted it this way.

(they travel through the countryside for a long time)

Lech: Look! A beautiful hill with a mighty oak tree on top!

Czech: What is that animal? Is it a bird?

Eagle: Squawk! Squawk!

Rus: Yes, it is a magnificent eagle. It is a lucky place. Let us stop here to rest. *(they rest)*

Lech: I must climb the tree with the eagle.

Eagle: Squawk! Squawk!

Czech: Good idea.

Rus: What can you see?

Lech: I can see lots of water to the north, hills and mountains to the south, flat fertile fields to the east, and thick, dark forest to the west.

Czech: Let us each go a different way to find new land. I will go south.

Rus: Good idea. I will go east.

Lech: And I will stay right here. What do you think, common people?

Common People: Some of us will go with Czech, some of us will go with Rus, but most of us want to stay right here with Lech.

Lech: And so it is done. Farewell, brothers, until we meet again.

(Lech, Czech and Rus slap hands, musketeer style)

Lech, Czech and Rus: Yo!

Eagle: Squawk! Squawk!

(All actors take a bow)

(12)

Jadwiga
and her
Apron of Roses

Jadwiga and her Apron of Roses

Summary

Some people will go to great lengths to help others and make sure they are fed and watered. Queen Jadwiga was one such person and, as legend has it, she hid food in her apron and sneaked out of her castle nightly to give to the poor.

Tale

Jadwiga was a devout Christian and was well known for her helpfulness and philanthropy, especially for the poor. In 1397 she founded a theological college in Krakow and also contributed to the restoration of the University of Krakow. Her impartiality, intelligence, and benevolence were widely respected.

Some said that Jadwiga was too young to be a Queen (at the age of 12) and that, as a child , was a mere "tool" to her advisors. Others said that she matured quickly and her good personality, charm and kindness were her strengths. Wikipedia refers to her as "the spirited mother of the poor, weak and ill in Poland".

She was a skilful mediator, whose temperament seemed tuned to reconciliation. As an example, when she accompanied her husband, the King, to Greater Poland, she was able to appease the local Lords who had shown hostility to the royals. On that same visit there was some disruption and damage to local peasants' property. Jadwiga was able to persuade her husband to compensate them, saying with compassion "we have, indeed, returned the peasants' cattle, but who can repair their tears?".

Jadwiga's charitable activities were many: she established schools, hospitals and churches, and promoted the use of the Polish language, especially in church services. She even ordered that the Bible be translated into Polish. Even after her death she was charitable: the sale of her jewellery paid for the complete restoration of the University of Krakow.

However, she is most famous for the tale of Jadwiga and her apron of roses. As a devout Christian, Jadwiga had a benevolent side and liked to help the poor. She often smuggled food (bread, meat and cheese) out of a secret door at the back of the royal castle. However, the King became suspicious and started to wonder where his wife was going each evening. This was fuelled by the King's advisors were spreading rumours that Jadwiga was taking secrets to rebels, enemies and those plotting against the monarchy. The King became angry and was determined to find out the truth.

So, one night as Jadwiga was leaving by the secret door, her husband confronted her and demanded to see what was in her apron. If she was carrying food for the poor then she would almost certainly be given the death sentence. But by some miracle, when she unravelled her apron there wasn't any food, but only a beautiful garland of roses. The King was very sorry that he had doubted her, and their relationship remained strong. Even to this day Jadwiga is depicted as wearing an apron of roses. It is quite amusing that most of the sources say that the King "sprang out of the bushes" in order to confront his wife!

However, Jadwiga's life had a sad ending. She died in 1399 at the age of just twenty-five shortly after giving birth to her only child (a daughter). They were buried together in Krakow and the shrine can be seen at Wawel Cathedral, Krakow, to this day.

Her short life has left a large footprint. She was one of the greatest and most benevolent rulers of Poland and oversaw perhaps the largest state in Central Eastern Europe at that time. She was beautified on 8th August 1986, and Canonised on 8th June 1997 and is the patron saint of Poland. Why not take a trip to Krakow and pay your respects to this famous and upstanding Queen?

Vocabulary

Do you know these words? Look them up in your dictionary if you don't.

devout – *devoted, committed*
philanthropy – *concern and help for the poor*
theological college – *school for theory and religion*
to restore – *to make good, especially buildings*
impartiality – *able to be a good judge of people and situations*
mediator – *someone who can help solve problems or arguments*
to appease – *to make happy*
peasants – *poor people, especially farmers*
to smuggle – *to take and give secretly*
garland of roses – *beautiful ring of roses*
footprint – *impact (on modern society)*
upstanding - *respectable*

Did you know?

❖ In the old days it was hard to get past the city walls after dark because there was a curfew;

❖ Jadwiga probably hid bread, vegetables and wine in her apron;

❖ The most popular foodstuffs in Poland are pork and beet vegetables, and the most popular alcoholic drinks are beer with raspberry juice, and vodka.

What do you think?

1. Was Jadwiga a good Queen to give to the poor?
2. If you were Jadwiga, what would you put in your apron?
3. Who is the kindest person you know?
4. If someone is very kind to the poor or sick, how should we thank them?
5. What is the kindest thing you have done for someone lately?

Play: Jadwiga and her Apron of Roses

Characters

Queen Jadwiga
King
God
Poor People

Setting

Just outside the Royal Palace, near the poor peoples' houses

Script

Poor People: We are hungry. We are sick. We are poor. We have no money.

God: Who will help them?

Queen Jadwiga: I will help them! *(Jadwiga gathers up some food and drink from the kitchen and puts it into her apron. She climbs over the palace wall)* Hello poor people! I have some food and drink for you.

Poor People: Oh, Queen Jadwiga! Thank you! *(the poor people eat and drink and have a merry party; Jadwiga sneaks away back to the palace)*

King: Hmmm, where does my wife go every night? Does she have a lover? I must find out.

Queen Jadwiga: My kitchen has lots of food and drink. Let me take some to the poor people again.

King: I will hide in the bushes. I will find out where my wife is going. I will surprise her. *(the King jumps from the bushes and surprises Jadwiga)* Surprise! What are you doing? Where are you going? Tell me now!

Queen Jadwiga: Oh, darling King, I am only taking these beautiful roses to the poor people. *(she opens her apron to reveal many many beautiful roses – but no food and no drink)*

Poor People: We are hungry. We are sick. We are poor. We have no money.

God: Who will help them?

Queen Jadwiga: I will help them! Here, have these beautiful roses!

Poor People: Thank you, Queen Jadwiga. We love you.

King: I'm sorry to doubt you, my dear. I love you too.

God: *(weeping)* Oh, I do love a happy ending!

(All actors take a bow)

Part 4

Places and Things

(13)

How the Pussy Willow got its Fur

How the Pussy Willow got its Fur

Summary

Some kittens fell into a river but were saved by some pussy willow trees who helped them back to shore.

Tale

Have you heard of the Pussy Willow Tree? It grows by the sides of rivers, lakes and streams. It has long, thin branches that appear to "sweep" and "weep" into the water. It is similar to a weeping willow tree, except that it is smaller and has soft, white buds on its thin branches. These branches swish in the breeze.

The tale goes that a mother cat was playing with her kittens at the water's edge. The kittens were young and cute, and they liked to chase butterflies. One day they were chasing butterflies when they fell into the river. Their mother started to cry. What could she do?

The willow trees heard the mother cat's cry and longed to help her. The trees swept their long branches into the river to rescue the kittens. The kittens held on tightly to the branches and were brought to shore.

The kittens were safe.

The tree is called the pussy willow because each springtime the white, soft buds on their branches remind us of this favour.

Vocabulary

Do you know these words? Look them up in your dictionary if you don't.

pussy – *children's name for a cat*
buds – *soft, white flowers, the shape of a small ball*
swish – *to move gently*
breeze – *light, gentle wind*
to chase – *to run after, to try to catch*
to rescue – *to save, bring to safety*
favour – *act of helpfulness*

Did you know?

- ❖ The longest river in Poland is the Vestula;
- ❖ The River Vestula runs through Krakow, Warsaw, and meets the Baltic Sea in Gdansk;
- ❖ Kittens, just like puppies, are born blind.

What do you think?

1. Can you swim?
2. Have you ever swum in a river?
3. What's the longest river in your country?
4. What's the longest river in the world?
5. If you saw a kitten in trouble in a river, what would you do?

Play: How the Pussy Willow got its Fur

Characters

Mother Cat
Kitten 1
Kitten 2
Kitten 3
Willow trees
River

Setting

A winding and freely-flowing river in the flat lowlands of Poland; willows line each bank.

Script

Mother Cat: Meow! Oh, what a lovely place. Let's stay here for a while. Kittens, you can play.
Kitten 1: Meow! Really? This is beautiful.
Kitten 2: Meow! Really? This is wonderful.
Kitten 3: Meow! Really? This is heaven. *(the kittens play with leaves and sticks by the water's edge)*
Mother Cat: Be careful, my little kittens, the water can come and go very quickly.
Kittens 12&3: We will be careful, mother! *(the kittens continue to play)*
River: I am the river. My waters come and go. Sometimes I am friendly, and sometimes I am rough. *(the river sweeps the kittens into the water)*
Kittens 12&3: Help! Help! We are in the water!
Mother Cat: Oh, no! What can I do? *(Mother cat looks on worried)*

Pussy Willow Trees: Don't worry, Mother Cat, we will help. *(the trees dangle their branches into the water)* Hold on to our branches and you will be safe.

Kittens 12&3: Meow! Thank you pussy willow tree.

Mother Cat: My kittens are safe!

Kittens 12&3: We are safe!

Pussy Willow Tree: And that is how the pussy willow got its fur.

(All actors take a bow)

(14)

What is the National Flower of Poland?

What is the National Flower of Poland?

Summary

There is an official national flower, the Corn Poppy (or red poppy). However, there are some other contenders, including sunflowers, roses, carnations, St John's Wort, and some more unusual flowers such as the Siberian Iris, Globe Flower, Ostrich Fern, or the elusive 'fire flower'.

Tale

There is an official national flower, the Corn Poppy (or red poppy) due to historic battles that occurred. However, there are some other contenders, too, including sunflowers, roses, carnations, St John's Wort, and some more unusual contenders such as the Siberian Iris, Globe Flower, or Ostrich Fern.

Let us look at some of the contenders.

The official national flower of Poland is the Corn Poppy (Papaver Rhoeas in Latin), and typically has a black 'button' centre and four or more red petals. They bloom in late spring. They are associated with battle and war, and in particular one story from the Second World War. It took place at a monastery called Monte Cassino in Italy. Whilst the Allies failed to take the position, it was finally the Poles under General Anders that secured the position. This was at a cost, though, and the 1,000 Polish casualties were echoed by the mountainside covered in red poppies. It was said that the hills were covered with Polish blood.

It also has significance from the First World War when fields that had seen battle were covered with red poppies. The bloom in late spring at these sites is remarkably beautiful.

Sunflowers are amazing in that such a tiny seed can produce such a tall and magnificent plant. JW Connolly writes an interesting anecdote about sunflower seeds. When the writer was a child they used to feed their pet rabbit with a kind of mix that resembled muesli that contained some stripy seeds which the writer later recognised as sunflower seeds. When first in Poland, the writer saw people in the street with huge bags of them, or even carrying a huge sunflower head from where they plucked the delicious seeds. In those days people everywhere from bus stations to pubs battled with and nibbled at them, just like the rabbit. The anecdote concludes "I would hate the thought of robbing more rabbits of the most tasty part of their meal". But a discussion thread on polishforums.com asks "would all Poles think of Poland when they see a sunflower?".

We previously came across Queen Jadwiga and her apron of roses, and so the rose has some claim as an important national flower.

Theflowerexpert.com notes some very rare varieties of flower that can be found in Poland, including the Siberian Iris, Globe Flower, Ostrich Fern, and the Broad Buckler Fern. More common are, for example, geraniums, pink amaryllis, crocuses, freesia, and alanya.

St John's Wort is an interesting contender: it has long been thought to be a mystical and magical plant. It is associated with Saint John the Baptist, and is often in full bloom on St. John's Day. Anything can happen on St. John's Eve, June 23rd. Apparently fairies appear on the night and can predict your future; mists are supposed to mark the entrances to the underworld; and herbs, stones and crystals take increasing power on that night. In British culture the night is portrayed in Shakespeare's 'A Midsummer Nights Dream' (1595).

The plant that captures my attention, though, is far more elusive: the 'fire flower'. What exactly this is, one can only speculate, but I imagine it to be a relative of the sunflower. If you look up "fire flower images" on Google then there are some really beautiful and unreal pictures. They depict flowers as if on fire, as if the plants, leaves and flowers themselves were growing in and breathing fire.

Concerning 'fire flowers', I could not find much information on them (though they certainly do exist). On Wikipedia a search for 'fire flowers' directs the reader to a brief page 'Polish folk beliefs', citing them as a part of Polish culture, and that the study of Polish folklore began in the nineteenth century. Are they a kind of sunflower? Maybe 'fire flower' is a nickname of some kind. My opinion is that fire flowers are some kind of sunflower, after all the sun is a big ball of fire (and the moon is made of cheese).

One cannot underestimate the significance of flowers in Polish culture: when invited to someone's house it is expected to give flowers to the lady of the house, and celebrations such as births and weddings are not considered complete without a good number of roses, lilies, carnations and orchids. One contributor to polishforums.com notes how some plants are connected with particular ceremonies or dates, for example the horse-chestnut flower is associated with end-of-school exams in May, or mistletoe for Christmas, or willows for Easter.

Vocabulary

Do you know these words? Look them up in your dictionary if you don't.

battles – *fights of war*

contender – *possible option, with a choice to be made*

Latin – *ancient Greek / Roman language*

to bloom – *to flower (verb)*

monastery – *a place where monks live*

The Allies – *the good countries in the Second World War*

casualty – *injury or death*

muesli – *alpine cereal made with nuts and oats*

to pluck – *to remove with two fingers*

to nibble – *to bite in small mouthfuls, like a rabbit*

mystical – *of mystery, we don't know*

to speculate – *to theorise, we don't really know*

nickname – *informal name*

Did you know?

❖ Sunflower oil is made from sunflowers, but oil can also be made from olives;

❖ Sunflowers can grow up to ten metres high;

❖ The most popular flowers for weddings are roses, lilies and carnations.

What do you think?

1. What is your favourite colour?
2. What does a fire flower look like?
3. What's your favourite flower?
4. How many flowers can you name?
5. How many different shapes of flower petal can you find?

Play: Fire Flowers

Characters

Fire Flower (FF)
Farmer (F)

Setting

A large, rolling field in Central Poland.

Script

Farmer: It's a hot day. I need some water.
Fire Flower: I need some water, too. I'm thirsty.
Farmer: I'm sorry? Can you speak?
Fire Flower: Yes, I can.
Farmer: Oh, nice to meet you.
Fire Flower: Nice to meet you, too.
Farmer: What are you?
Fire Flower: I'm a fire flower.
Farmer: A fire flower? Really?
Fire Flower: Yes, and I'm very thirsty. Can you find me some water?
Farmer: Sure. *(the farmer goes to the river and gets some water)* Here you are.
Fire Flower: Thank you. *(drinks)* That's better.
Farmer: OK, fire flower. See you later.
Fire Flower: OK, farmer, see you later.
(Later...)
Farmer: A talking flower? It can't be. Well, it is a very hot day!

(All actors take a bow)

(15)

The
Three Gifts

The Three Gifts

Summary

There is a long tale about the fate of a sister, a step-sister, a step-brother and a wicked step-mother who, through fate and fortune, get involved with the royal family with differing fortunes.

Tale

There was once a wicked step-mother who took care of three children. The first was her own daughter who despite being bad-tempered and vain was much favoured. The second was her step-daughter and, although she had great beauty, was despised by her step-mother. Similarly the third child, a step-son, was also treated badly and given no favours. Often the daughter was favoured at the two step-children's expense.

The first fateful event happened one Sunday morning as the step-daughter was picking flowers for church. As she looked up after picking the flowers, she saw in front of her three young men clothed in robes of dazzling white. Next to them stood an old man, who came to the step-daughter to ask for coins. She felt calmed by the old man and gave him her last coin. The old man put his hand on the girl's head and said to the three youths "You see this orphan, she is good. She gave her last coin to us. What do you wish for her?".

The first of the youths wished that when she cried her tears would turn to pearls. The second wished that when she laughed, roses would fall from her lips. The third wished that when she touched water, golden fish would spring from it. And so it was.

The following Sunday the wicked step-mother sent her own daughter into the garden to pick flowers in the hope of a similar result. However, the old man and the youths seemed to sense that the daughter was insincere. The first youth wished that when she cried her tears would turn to lizards! The second wished that when she laughed, toads would fall from her lips! And the third wished that when she touched water it would be filled with serpents! And so it was!

Soon after, the step-son had had enough of his miserable life at home and set out on his own to seek his fortune. He was able to find an honest job as a servant in a palace. A day came that the brother sat by a brook in the palace gardens holding a picture of his lost sister and crying. The King saw him and asked who the portrait was of. Of course, it was a portrait of his long-lost sister. The King declared that such a beautiful girl should also come to work at the palace, and instructed the boy to write a letter to his step-mother asking that the girl be sent straight away to be married to the King.

To cut a long story short, the evil step-mother received the letter and plotted that her own daughter should take the place of her step-daughter and marry the King. And so the daughter and the King married.

Unfortunately for the step-daughter she chanced to cry, laugh and touch water at the ceremony, whereupon there was a deluge of lizards, toads and serpents! The King thought that the boy had tricked him, and struck him unconscious. At that moment the step-daughter ran in and explained that she was the boy's beloved sister, not the other girl.

The daughter and the step-daughter came running, and with the help of a magic potion the boy came back to life. The evil step-mother was banished, and the others lived happily ever after.

Vocabulary

Do you know these words? Look them up in your dictionary if you don't.

step-mother – *not the natural mother*
vain – *untruthful, fake*
despised – *not liked, hated*
fateful – *according to fate, pre-determined event*
dazzling white – *shiny bright white*
orphan – *child without a mother or father*
to wish – *to dream for something good, often with eyes closed*
toad – *ugly frog*
serpent – *poisonous snake*
brook – *small stream or river*
portrait – *small painted picture of a person*
to plot – *to plan in a bad way*
potion – *magic medicine*
to banish – *to send away, exile*

Did you know?

❖ Portraits can either be very small (as in this story) or very big, like on the walls of a palace;
❖ Orphans often end up being cared for by the Church in an orphanage;
❖ It is an old custom to let a child take their pick of three wrapped and unseen gifts. The three gifts may or may not be of equal value

What do you think?

1. Who is your favourite character in the story? Why?
2. Who is your least favourite character in the story? Why?
3. Do step-children have a hard time of it?
4. Do you find it easy or difficult to make choices?
5. Have you ever had to make a difficult choice between three equally attractive or unattractive options?

Play script: The Three Gifts

Characters

Step-Mother
Daughter
Step-Daughter
Step-Son
Old Man
Three Young Men
King
Palace Servants

Setting

Rolling polish countryside, with a small village and the King's palace.

Script

Scene 1: (in the house)

Step-Mother: Ha ha! He he! I am the wicked step-mother!
Daughter: And I am the wicked step-mother's daughter! My mother loves me.
Step-Mother: I love her. I adore her.

Step-Daughter: I am the step-daughter. My wicked step-mother hates me.

Step-Mother: Clean the kitchen! Make the beds! Tidy your room! Wash the dishes!

Step-Daughter: Yes, yes...

Step-Son: I am the step-son. My wicked step-mother hates me too.

Step-Mother: Clean the bathroom! Sweep the floor! Wash the windows! Take out the rubbish!

Step-Son: Yes, yes...

Scene 2 (in the garden near the church)

Step-Mother: Go out and pick some flowers for church, you stupid girl!

Step-Daughter: Yes, wicked step-mother. *(she picks some flowers,* and an old man and three handsome young men appear)

Old Man: Hello, young lady. What are you doing?

Step-Daughter: I am picking beautiful flowers for my wicked step-mother.

Old Man: Really? Hmmm... *(he thinks)* Here are three young men. What do you wish for this poor girl?

Young Man 1: I wish that when she cries, her tears turn to pearls.

Young Man 2: I wish that when she laughs, roses fall from her lips.

Young Man 3: I wish that when she touches water, golden fish will spring from it.

Old Man: And so it shall be.

Step-Mother: It's true! Look! Pearls, roses and golden fish! I will send my own daughter out and she will be able to do the same! Darling daughter, please go out and pick some flowers for church, my angel.

Daughter: Yes, dear mother. *(she picks some flowers, and an old man and three handsome young men appear again)*

Old Man: Hello, young lady. What are you doing?

Daughter: I am picking beautiful flowers for my dear mother.

Old Man: Really? Hmmm... *(he thinks)* Here are three young men. What do you wish for this girl?

Young Man 1: I wish that when she cries, her tears turn to lizards!

Young Man 2: I wish that when she laughs, toads fall from her lips!

Young Man 3: I wish that when she touches water, it will be filled with serpents!

Old Man: And so it shall be.

Step-Mother: Oh, no, what evil is happening? Lizards, toads and serpents! Ahhhhhh!!!!!

Scene 3 (at the Royal Palace)

King: I am lonely. I need a wife. Who shall I marry? Hmmm *(he thinks)*. Servants, bring me two young women from the village. I will choose one to marry.

Servants: Yes, your Majesty. *(the servants go out and come back a short time later with the Daughter and Step-Daughter)* Here are two young ladies from the village, as you asked, your Majesty.

King: Very good. *(he looks at the Step-Daughter)* Say your name, sing and dance!

Step-Daughter: My name is Step-Daughter. *(she sings and dances, and pearls, roses and golden fish appear)*.

King: Very good. *(he looks at the Daughter)* Say your name, sing and dance!

Daughter: My name is Daughter. *(she sings and dances, but lizards, toads and serpents appear)*.

King: My goodness! Oh. No! I have no choice! I must marry the first girl!

Step-Son: Thank goodness!

(the King and Step-Daughter hug, and live happily ever after).

(All actors take a bow)

(16)

The Legend
of the
Golden Duck

The Legend of the Golden Duck

Summary

A talking duck gives money to Jacob on condition that he only spends it on himself. However, he gives one gold coin to a poor beggar upon which all his wealth and goods disappear.

Tale

Long ago in Warsaw there was a young man, Jacob, who was known for his revelry and enjoyment of fun parties. He often told stories and jokes, and everyone liked him. However, there was no money to be made from his jokes and revelry: he was poor.

So, he had nothing to lose.

One day he decided enough was enough. He decided to search for the golden duck and his fortune.

What was the golden duck? It was a magical bird that lived in an underground pond way beneath the Ostrogoski Palace. Jacob found the palace in a valley. He soon realised it was uninhabited because in the evening there was no candlelight at the windows. So, the next day he went in to explore.

He went into the palace's dark cellar – room after room of dark, musty cellars... until he came across a cave, deep underground.

What do you think he found? That's right – a golden duck! What's more, the golden duck spoke! "Hello", it said, as it glided about the water. It had fine feathers and a crest (a crown of feathers).

"Hello, golden duck" said Jacob. The golden duck replied. It explained that Jacob would be given one hundred ducats (gold coins) which he had to spend that day, and only on himself.

With his purse of one hundred ducats he started his spending spree. He bought new clothes and ate in the most expensive restaurant. The only things he had to do was keep his secret about the golden duck to himself and only spend the money on himself.

But his dreams started to get the better of him.

He looked into his purse. Only one gold coin remained. He decided to buy a cup of the finest wine, and with no money left , go back to the golden duck and claim his next one hundred ducats. However, on his way he came across a poor beggar and, as you can probably guess, gave his last gold coin to the beggar.

Suddenly, with a bang and a flash, the golden duck appeared and chanted a rhyme:

"You did not keep your word, nor our deal,
when you gave the poor beggar a meal.
And today, though you are in great need,
a poor life once again you shall lead.
Now, the goods that my gold for you bought,
In the blink of an eye will now come to nought"

Jacob could not believe his eyes. His beautiful clothes vanished, and all the fine things he had bought disappeared. Can you believe it? Jacob was left standing in his old rags once more. According to polish4kids.com, he looked at the beggar who said:

"Your good-heartedness has triumphed over greed and true treasure is not enchanted gold but a generous spirit and a pair of hands eager to work. That is the way to gain a fortune and the goodwill of others."

Jacob took this advice and worked hard to become a fine shoemaker. In fact, he made the best shoes in all of Warsaw.

To commemorate this, the people of Warsaw built a fountain in the image of the golden duck. To this day you can see this fountain (albeit a replica) in the courtyard of the palace. The enchanted golden lake is said to be way underground below it, apparently.

Vocabulary

Do you know these words? Look them up in your dictionary if you don't.

revelry – *party and enjoyment*
uninhabited – *nobody lives there*
to explore – *to look around (and find treasure?)*
cellar – *storage rooms below a building*
purse – *money bag*
to vanish – *to disappear*
enchanted - *magical*

Did you know?

❖ In China, a tiger is a symbol of wealth, especially if you dream about it;
❖ Gold coins in Europe were originally called 'ducats', for example in Shakespeare's play 'The Merchant of Venice';
❖ In many countries people invest in gold rather than put money in the bank.

What do you think?

1. If a golden duck offered you 100 gold coins, would you accept?
2. Do you think Jacob was foolish to accept the duck's offer?
3. In some countries a duck is a lucky animal. What is a lucky animal in your country?
4. What's your favourite animal? Why?
5. What noise does a duck make? What noises do other animals make in your country?

Play: The Legend of the Golden Duck

Characters

Jacob
Jacob's Friends
The Golden Duck
A Poor Beggar

General Setting

In and around the castle and the cobbled streets of Warsaw, long ago.

Script

Scene 1: A Pub

Jacob: Let me tell you another story... Did you hear the one about the... An even funnier joke is...
Jacob's Friends: Ha ha, he he, ho ho, Jacob, you're so funny!
Jacob: Thankyou very much. But did you ever hear the funny story about the Golden Duck... Hmmm... *(he thinks to himself...) the Golden Duck...Hmmm...*

Scene 2: Ostrogoski Palace

Jacob: No-one lives in this tired old building. I will go inside. I will try to find the Golden Duck. *(he walks carefully and cautiously into the ruined building, and into the cellar)* So many rooms, so dark, so musty... will I ever find the Golden Duck?

(suddenly...)

Golden Duck: Hello! I am the Golden Duck! Quack!

Jacob: Hello, Golden Duck. My name is Jacob.

Golden Duck: Yes, I know. Quack!

Jacob: You know?

Golden Duck: I know everything. I am not stupid. I am very clever. Quack!

Jacob: Oh, OK. Can you help me make my fortune?

Golden Duck: Yes, of course. Take this purse of one hundred gold pieces. You must spend it all today, and only on yourself, Jacob. Come back tomorrow and I will give you another one hundred gold pieces. Understand?

Jacob: Understood.

Golden Duck: Be gone! Quack!

Scene 3: A Fine Restaurant, A Fine Shop

Jacob: Ha ha! Look at all this delicious food! Look at all these wonderful clothes! I will never be poor again!

Jacob's Friends: *(they look in through the window)* Ha ha, he he, ho ho, Jacob, you're so funny!

Scene 4: The Street

Jacob: Ho! I have just one gold coin left.

Poor Beggar: Hello, son. I am a poor beggar. Won't you help me? I am hungry.

Jacob: But I can't give you my last gold coin. The Golden Duck will be angry.

Poor Beggar: Golden Duck? Ha ha, he he, ho ho! Oh, son, you're so funny!

Jacob: Alright, poor beggar. Here is my last gold coin. Go and buy some food.

Poor Beggar: Thank you, son. *(he leaves)*

(suddenly – a big flash)

Golden Duck: Jacob! You betray me? Why did you give your last gold coin to that poor beggar? I told you *only* to spend it on yourself!

Jacob: Yes, but... but... but...

Golden Duck: All your fine clothes – be gone! All your delicious food – be gone! And all your money and wealth – be gone! *(suddenly all Jacob's fine things disappear in a flash, and he is left standing in his old rags)*

Jacob's Friends: Oh, Jacob, there you are! Where have you been? Another party? Come on, come with us, it's time for a drink in the pub.

Jacob: But I met a Golden Duck, and she gave me 100 gold coins, and...

Jacob's Friends: Ha ha, he he, ho ho, Jacob, you're so funny!

(All actors take a bow)

References

Nb. All internet references are http://www. unless otherwise indicated.

Introduction

anglik.net/polish_legends.htm
en.oxforddictionaries.com/definition/
https://en.wikipedia.org/wiki/Myth
http://dictionary.cambridge.org/dictionary/english/
dictionary.com/browse
merrian-webster.com/dictionary/
urbandictionary.com/define.php?term=skit
yourdictionary.com

The Dragon of Krakow

anglik.net/polish_legends.htm
polishtoledo.com/pagan/myths.htm

Obra Water Monster

anglik.net/polish_legends.htm

Rusalka

polishtoledo.com/pagan/myths.htm

The Mermaid of Warsaw

inyourpocket.com/warsaw/The-Story-of-Syrenka
polishtoledo.com/pagan/myths.htm
polish4kids.com-zone/legends

King Boleslaw and His Knights

anglik.net/polish_legends.htm

The Queen of the Baltic

polishtoledo.com/pagan/myths.htm

The Legend of Wanda

anglik.net/polish_legends.htm
polishtoledo.com/pagan/myths.htm

The Sleeping Knights

http://info-poland-buffalo.edu/classroom/legends/

Janosik: Polish Robin Hood

iarelactive.com/history/janosik.htm
krykiet.com/janosik_robin_hood.htm

The Trumpeter of Krakow

anglik.net/polish_legends.htm
info-poland.buffalo.edu/classroom/legends/
Kelly. E.P. (1928) *The Trumpeter of Krakow* (publisher unknown)
polish4kids.com/kids-zone/legends
wikipedia.com

The Three Brothers

info-poland.buffalo.edu/classroom/legends/
polish4kids.com/kids-zone/legends
http://slavorum.org/ancient-polish-legend-about-3-slavic-brothers-lech-czech-and-rus

Jadwiga and Her Apron of Roses

angelfire.com/mi4/polcit/LegendJadwiga.html
http://docslide.us/documents/polish-myths-and-legends.html

liquisearch.com/Jadwiga_of_poland/legends_and_veneration
polish4kids.com/kids-zone/legends/
vbvm.org/tour/Jadwiga-view.html
wikipedia.com

How the Pussy Willow got its Fur

polishtoledo.com/pagan/myths.htm

What is the National Flower of Poland?

https://polishforums.com/archives/2005-2009/life/poland-flower-representative-27658/
Shakespeare, W. (XXXX) *A Midsummer Night's Dream* (publisher unknown)
http://talesofenglishman.blogspot.com/2007/08/polish-passion-for-sunflower-seeds.html
theflowerexpert.com/content/flowerbusiness/flowersandsellers/national-native-popular-flowers-of-poland
wikipedia.com

The Three Gifts

brantfordpolish.com/tales/
http://eflinspell.com/GoldenrodThreeGifts.html

The Legend of the Golden Duck

https://cop19warsaw.wordpress.com
polarcenter.com
polish4kids.com/kids-zone/legends/

About the Author

Born and educated in the United Kingdom, Barry Nicholson holds a Masters degree in Teaching English as a Foreign Language from the University of Reading. During his career abroad, he has taught in the Far East, Germany, Turkey and Poland. His first book 'Practical English Summercamp Activities' was published in June 2015.
He currently lives in Krakow, Poland.

From the same author

Practical English Summercamp Activities

Published June 2015

ISBN: 9780993243806

If you want to ensure your students are not just parroting the right answers but actually absorbing the lessons you're teaching them, then allow educator Barry Nicholson to reveal his proven educational method:

ACTIVE FUN + LEARNING = SUCCESS

Whether you're teaching English as a foreign language or working with students who have special needs, this book provides you with more than one hundred enjoyable ways to engage your students in the classroom. Better yet, each activity leaves room for your own creative adjustments and can be adapted to fit your lessons.

Student participation is essential in any educational environment, and with this invaluable resource, you can make learning fun and easy for you and your students!

From the same author

Famous Tales From Turkey With Activities For The Primary Classroom

Published July 2015

ISBN: 8780993243813

Most of us have heard of the Wooden Horse of Troy, Saint Nicholas, or King Midas and his golden touch. But do you know that they all come from what is modern-day Turkey?

Educator Barry Nicholson shares twelve tales from Turkey's long and rich history, designed to enliven your class or project work.

Each unit can be used on its own or as a starting point for further study. Importantly, there are three suggested activities at the end of each section, designed to link the stories to practical activities for the classroom.

The activities will bring the tales to life and encourage children to engage with the story.

From the same author

Famous Tales From Britain With Activities For The Primary Classroom

Published January 2016

ISBN: 9780993243820

Does the Loch Ness Monster really exist? Who were Henry VIII's six wives? When was the London Underground built? And why is Weston-super-Mare so dismal?

Educator Barry Nicholson shares twelve tales from Britain's long and rich history, designed to enliven your class or project work.

Importantly, there are three suggested activities at the end of each section, designed to link the story to practical activities for the classroom. The activities bring the tales to life and encourage children to engage with the story.

These are tales of royalty; these are tales of mystery; these are tales of history; these are tales of tradition. These are the *Famous Tales From Britain*.

From the same author

Fun Activities For Primary Children

Published February 2016

ISBN: 9780993243837

Planning a party, summer camp or extra-curricular class? Then you'll need some fun activities to liven things up and allow your children to participate and interact in a creative and informal atmosphere.

This is especially true for primary-aged learners who speak English as their second language (ESL).

The materials in this book are designed to help children learn and apply the English language in an active environment. With this invaluable resource you can make learning FUN and EASY for you and your children!

From the same author
(upcoming)

Britain in Play: Stories and Skits for ESL

BRITAIN is a fascinating and diverse country, ideally located in Western Europe. In this book you will find sixteen stories from Britain's rich cultural history.

Read about King Henry VIII and his six wives, the murder of Thomas Becket in Canterbury, efforts to save London during the Blitz, and the rise and fall of The Beatles and MerseyBeat, among others.

Importantly, each story is accompanied by a play script designed for young learners.

Children and teens will enjoy acting out the skits, and will wake up to the joys of British stories through practical drama and literature.

The book is due for publication in June 2017.

www.ingramcontent.com/pod-product-compliance
Lightning Source LLC
Chambersburg PA
CBHW080550030426
42337CB00024B/4819